Socks Says!

By
CAROLYN BOGART FINCH

Illustrated By

Jack Barrows

BOGART COMMUNICATIONS INC.
Danbury, Connecticut

**SOCKS SAYS®! is a registered trademark of
BOGART COMMUNICATIONS INC.**

Address correspondence to
Carolyn Finch, professional speaker, author,
trainer and consultant.
51 Cedar Drive, Danbury, Connecticut 06811
203-792-4833

Illustrator-Artist Jack Barrows
55 Hospital Avenue, Danbury, Connecticut 06810
203-744-1527

Calligraphy by Allison Hulme

All rights reserved. No part of this book may be
reproduced or transmitted in any form or by any means,
electronic or mechanical, including photocopying, recording,
or by any information storage and retrieval system,
without permission in writing of the publisher.

Copyright 1993 by Carolyn Bogart Finch
and Jack Barrows
ISBN 1-882956-00-1 Soft Cover
ISBN 1-882956-01-X Hard Cover

This book is dedicated to the
President Bill Clinton family
and all families
everywhere

Also by Carolyn Finch

Universal Handtalk
Universal Handtalk Pocketguide
Portraits of Sounds
Survival Sign System

BOGART COMMUNICATIONS INC.
Danbury, Connecticut

Socks Says!

Just an ordinary cat this you might say,

Who happened to enter the Clinton household one day.

A tomcat with patches and paws pure white,

And shiny fur as black as the night.

How silly he thought those photographers are,

Snapping pictures while on their.........tummies

And sneaking around a car.

It's fun, it's different!

I never thought life could be this strange.

Just as I got settled in Little Rock

Then I had to change.

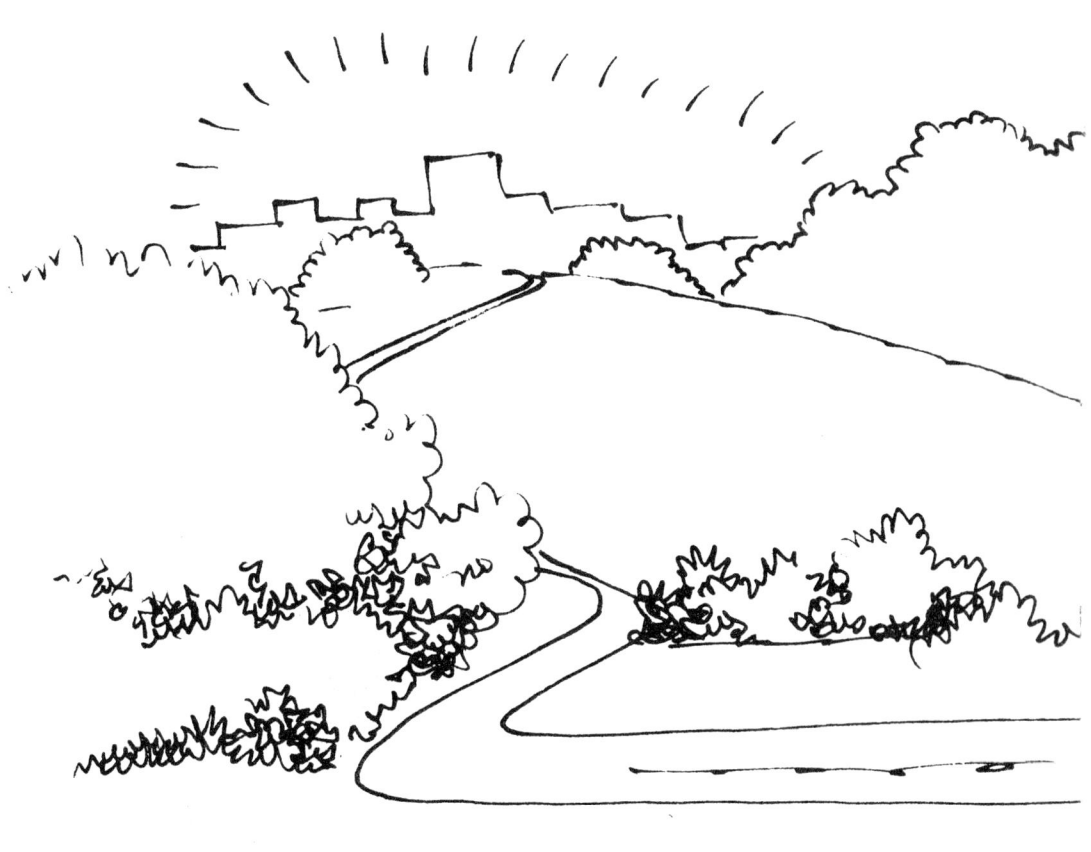

Like all God's creatures I just need food, love and a home.

And someone to spend time with and smooth my fur... with a comb.

I know there are poor cats who live in alleys,

With pending death and disease.

They have some human companions to pet them,
   And share garbage food if they please.

I speak to all cats: in the city, the country and up a tree.

You must care for yourself, groom yourself and

Strive for all you can be.

Do your best to get away from the alley,

Work hard to learn all you can know.

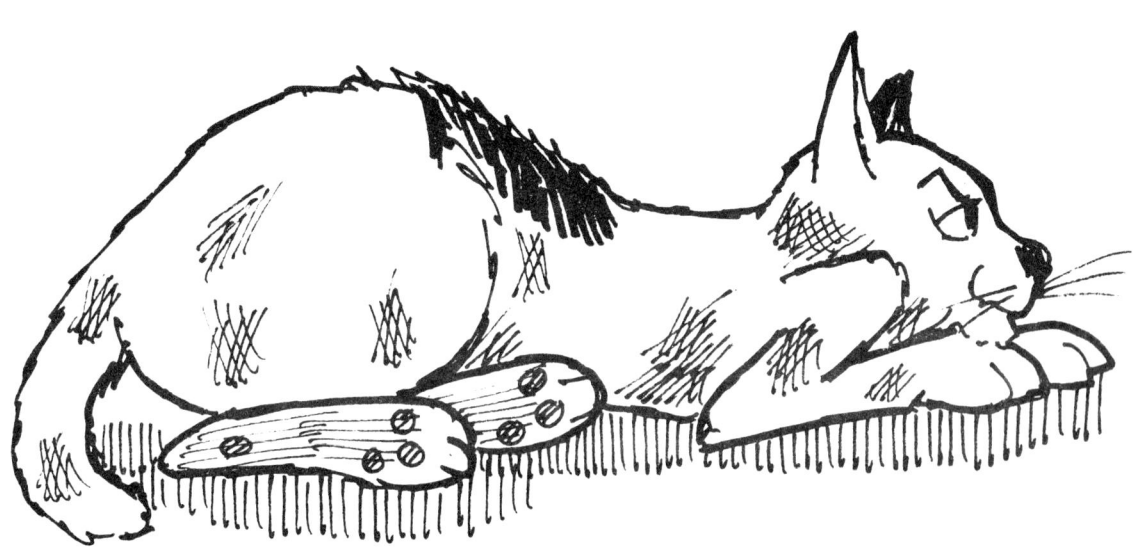

Keep yourself active and caring,

And who knows where you might go!

Perhaps you'll live in a mobile home,

An apartment or a house.

But wherever you are give your love,
your purrs, your meows,

And even give up your mouse.

Once you start to be there for others
"in need."

You will be highly thought of

And very... important indeed.

People will point to you, take pictures too.

You will be a part of a family,

    That has lots of love for you.

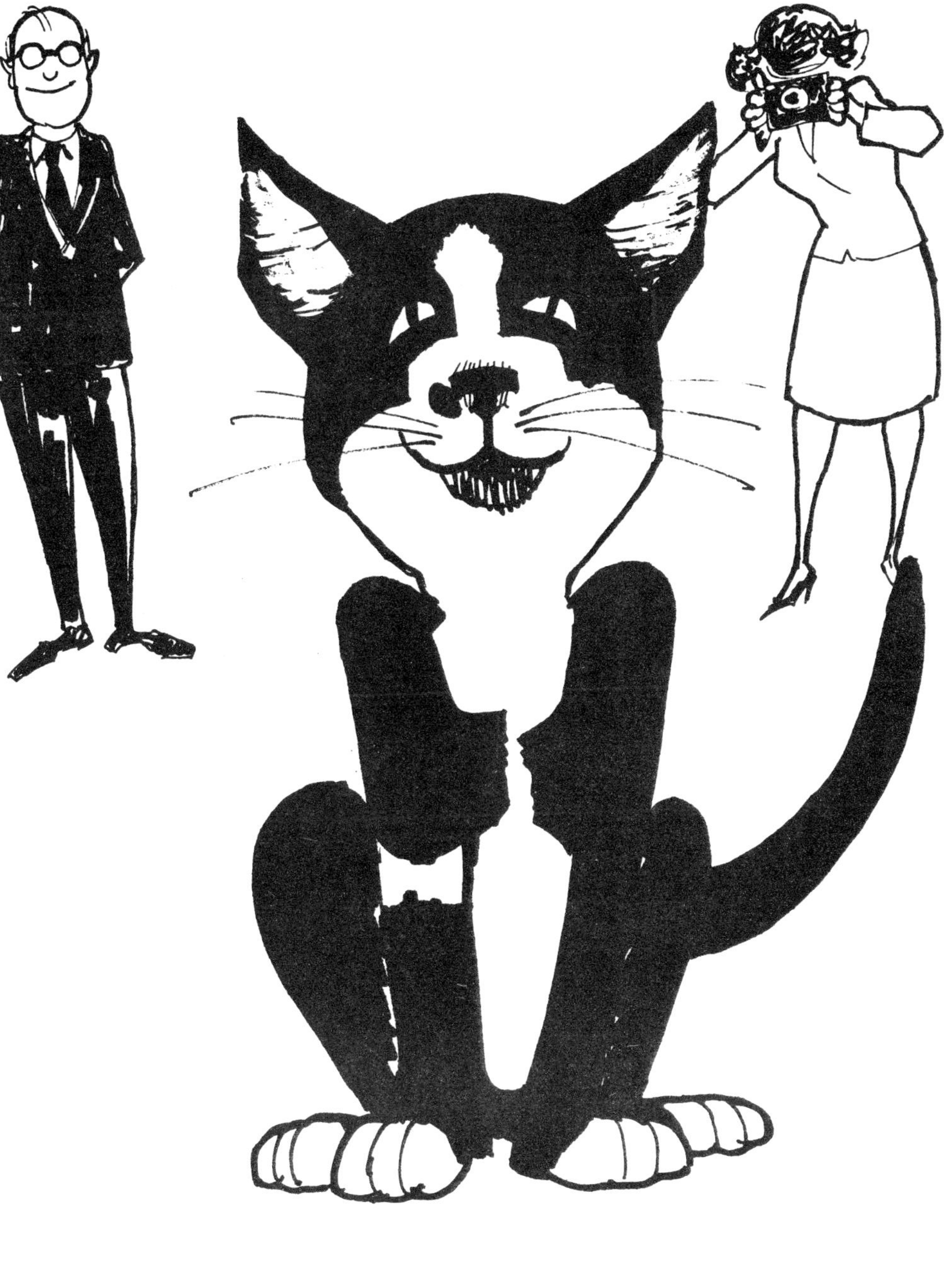

Some will hug you and kiss you on the head,

Sometimes they might let you sleep on their bed.

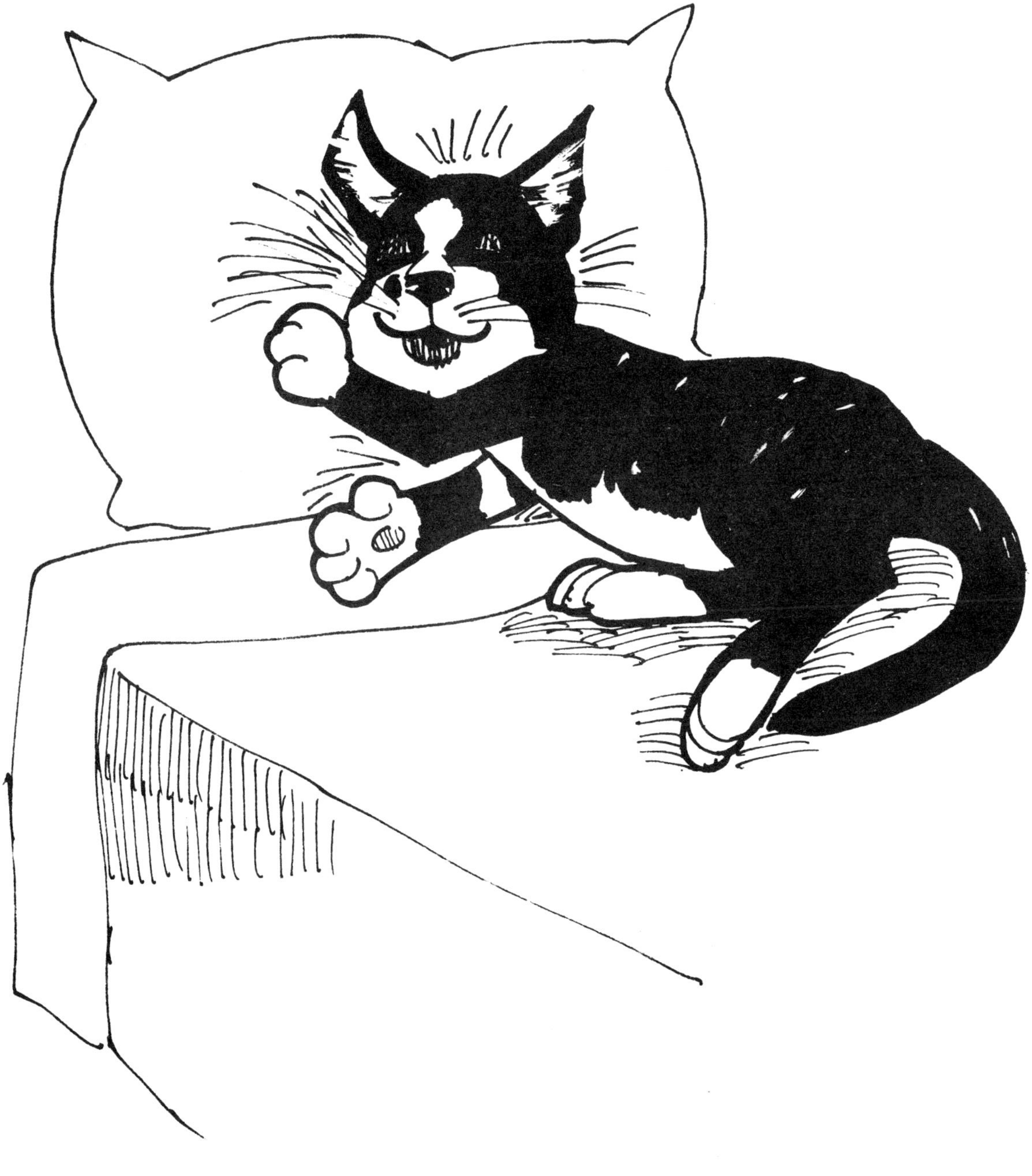

So get up on your feet, get started today,
To change your life in some special way.

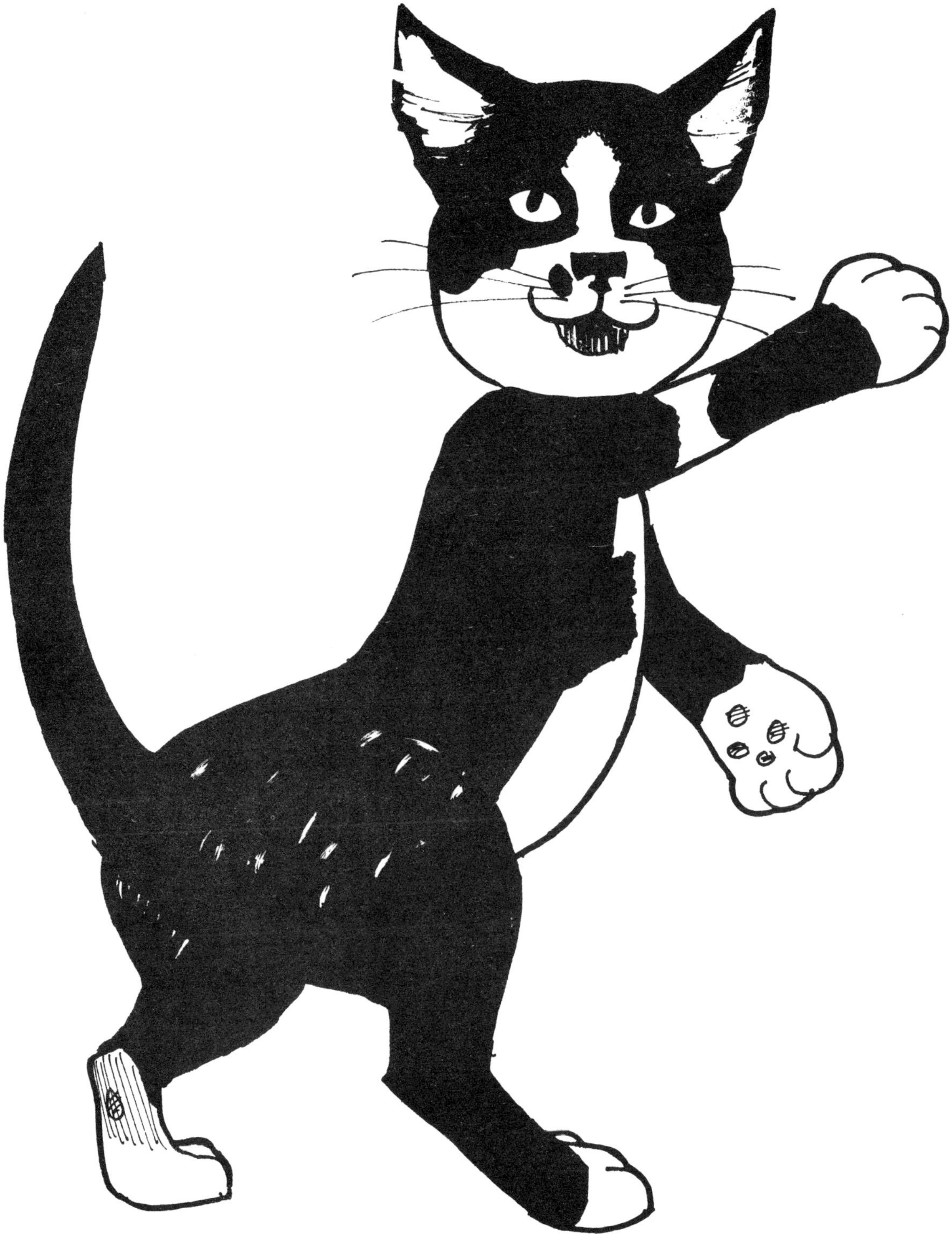

Spruce up, clean up and walk with style,

Then stop by and visit me once in a while.

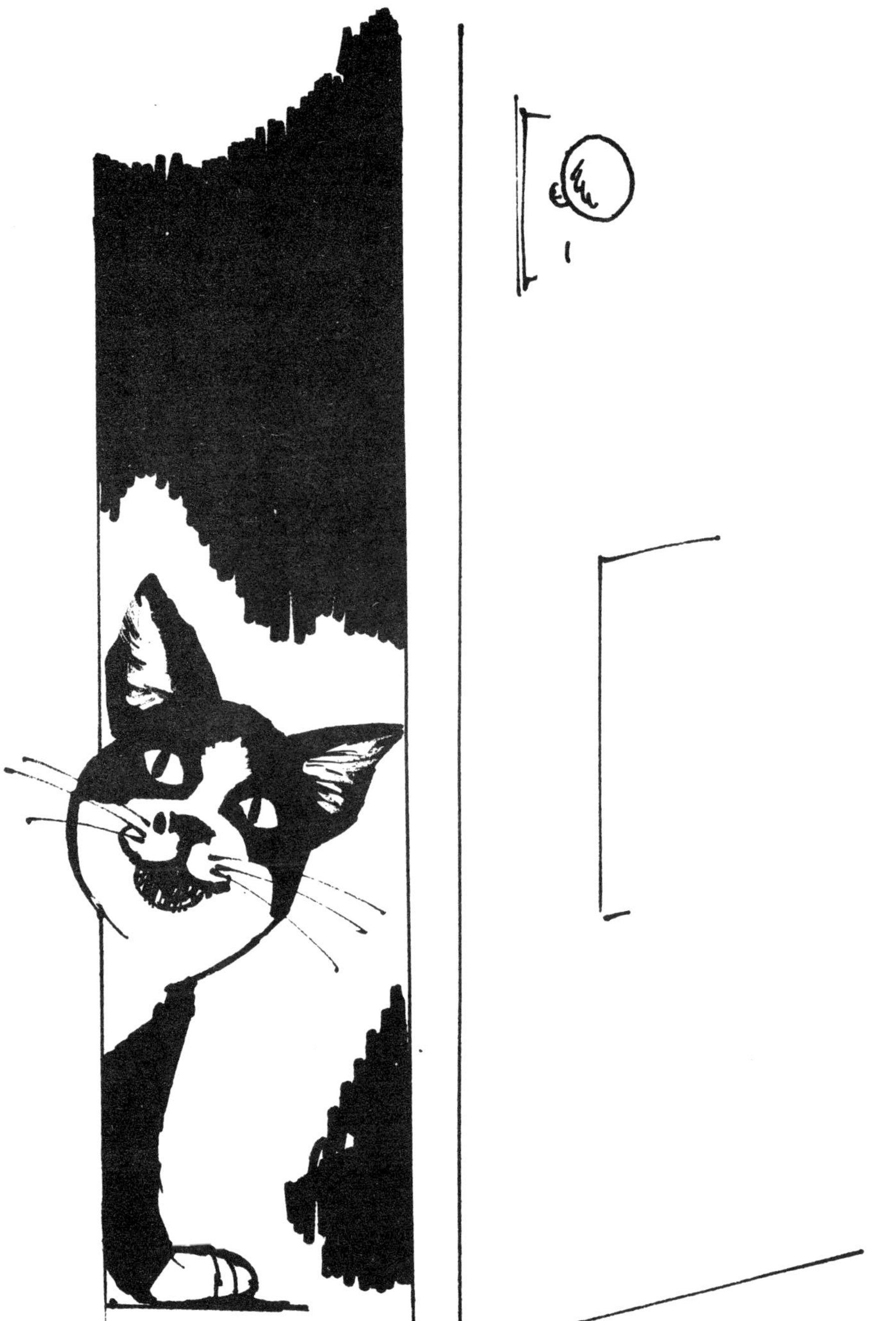

Carolyn Bogart Finch, author of <u>Socks Says</u>! is a professional speaker, speech pathologist and educator who has been creating poetry and telling stories for several years whether with her preschool children at Peter Piper School (the first school to mainstream handicapped children in Connecticut) or in her speech clinics, college classes or adult education programs. She has her B.S. In Early Childhood Education and Speech/Language Pathology from Elmira College and her M.S. in Communication from Western Connecticut State University. Ms. Finch has started over a dozen businesses including speech clinics and mail order sales operations. Recently she was an organizer and director for a bank for foreign speaking in her town of Danbury, Connecticut. She is creator of <u>Universal Handtalk</u>, a system of gestures to use in emergency situations, for educationally challenged and foreign speaking. She is featured in <u>Creative Innovators</u>, and is named in Who's Who of American Women. She combines her 30 plus years in Education, Health Care and Business for customized consulting and speeches to corporations, educational institutions and associations. Ms. Finch lives in Danbury, Connecticut with her husband, market researcher Donald Hulme.

Jack Barrows, illustrator, cartoonist and artist, demonstrates in **Socks Says!** his ability to make thoughts come alive through his pen & ink illustrations. Mr. Barrows, a longtime resident of Connecticut, served in the U.S. Navy and attended the Ringling School of Art in Sarasota, Florida, before embarking on his art career. He has been perfecting his skills for many years in a variety of media, including pen & ink, watercolor and acrylics. In addition to his work as a technical illustrator in corporate settings and as a visual materials specialist in an urban school system, Mr. Barrows has taught drawing and cartooning to both children and adults. His first contact with the White House occurred when he was invited to paint wooden eggs for the annual Easter Egg Roll during the past two administrations. These eggs have become part of a permanent Easter egg collection at the Smithsonian. Mr. Barrows is presently a freelance artist and book illustrator, having illustrated **Smart Selling**, **Universal Handtalk Pocketguide** and **You and Your Slipped Disc**. He is well known for his pen & ink drawings of many of Danbury's historical buildings and for his cartoon portraits drawn at parties and special events. He lives with his wife, Charlotte, in a 100 year old house in Danbury.

The End